Australian Geographic

DISCOVER

AUSSIE REPTILES

CONTENTS

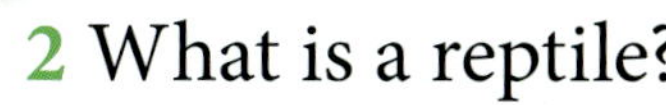

WHAT IS A REPTILE?

Lizards, snakes, crocodiles and turtles are all reptiles. They are **VERTEBRATE** animals covered in scales or bony plates. Scales are made of keratin – the same material as your fingernails. Reptiles can't control their body temperature by internal **THERMOREGULATION**.

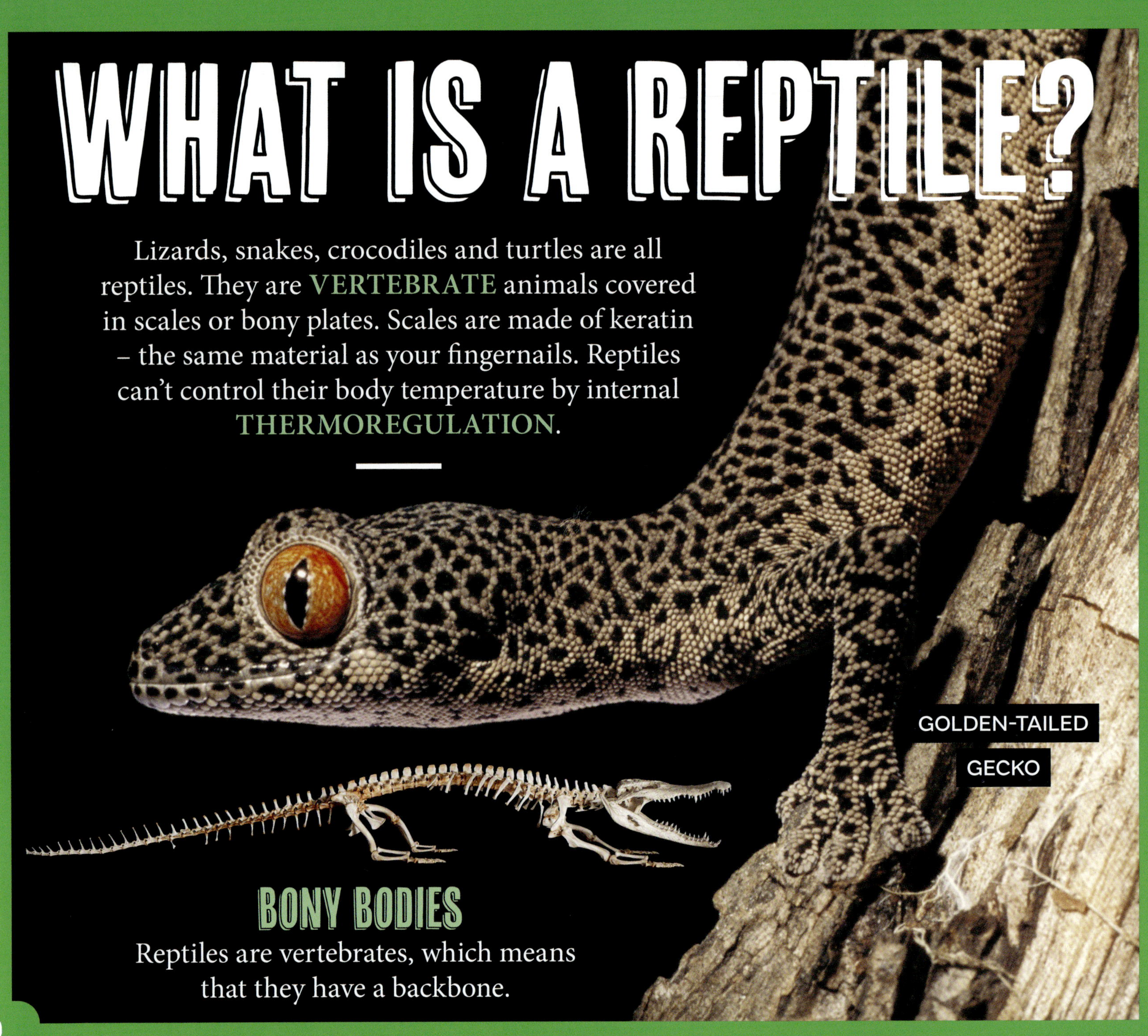

GOLDEN-TAILED GECKO

BONY BODIES

Reptiles are vertebrates, which means that they have a backbone.

Reptiles have existed for more than 300 million years, and they now live on every continent except Antarctica. There are more than 1000 species of reptile in Australia.

Australia has many **VENOMOUS** snakes, but we also have snakes that aren't venomous, like Stimson's python.

Not all reptiles have feet, but the ones that do have claws on their toes.

DID YOU KNOW?
The word reptile comes from a Latin word that means 'to creep'.

Reptiles are often seen basking in the sun, which warms them up.

STAYING WARM

Reptiles are **ECTOTHERMS** that don't maintain their body heat through bodily actions like shivering or panting. Instead, they regulate their body temperature by finding warm or cool places to rest.

To move or digest food, reptiles need to be warm. If a reptile gets too hot or cold, its body may stop working properly. To alter its temperature, a reptile may bask in the warm sun or hide in the cool shade.

INLAND TAIPAN

Small lizards find it very hard to control their temperature, especially those that live in the desert. Many desert-dwelling reptiles retreat into burrows during the hottest part of the day, sometimes borrowing those dug by other animals.

SMOOTH KNOB-TAILED GECKO

CHANGING COLOURS

Bearded dragons are able to alter their body temperature by changing the colour of their scaly skin. They become darker in cool weather so they can collect more warmth from the sun.

BEARDED DRAGON

REPTILE SKIN

As they grow, reptiles shed their skin or the plates (called scutes) covering their body. As the outer layer of skin dies, it must come off to make way for the new skin growing underneath. This is also called shedding. Young reptiles shed more often than older ones because they are growing more quickly.

Most snakes shed their entire skin in one piece like a sock. Underneath is a clean, fresh skin that fits perfectly.

GREEN TREE PYTHON

DID YOU KNOW?

Lizards shed their skin in pieces. Some lizards even eat the dead skin.

Turtles shed in pieces rather than all at once. A turtle's shell is made of bone, which is covered in protective scutes. Shedding the scutes piece by piece means that the turtle avoids rot and infection that can occur from being in the water.

Red-eared slider turtles are originally from North America, but have been introduced to Australia.

REPTILE EGGS

Most baby reptiles are born on land. Some reptiles give birth to live young, but most lay eggs. The eggs can be soft or hard, depending on which animal laid them. Soft-shelled eggs usually have a **LEATHERY** covering that helps keep the young reptiles safe from bad weather or **PREDATORS** in the wild.

KEELBACK SNAKE

Most baby reptiles have a special tooth or growth, called an egg tooth, that helps them to break free of the egg. When the time is right, they use the egg tooth to crack the shell from the inside and then push their way out.

Many snakes lay eggs, but some give birth to live young called snakelets. An egg-laying female snake will lay in a place that is humid and safe from predators. The number of eggs depends on the type of snake. Some snakes lay only a few; others as many as 100 eggs. Pythons coil their body around their eggs to keep them at the right temperature.

When a female turtle lays eggs, she buries them in sand, soil or among plants. Some turtles lay more than 100 eggs at a time. After the turtle lays her eggs, she returns to the sea and swims away.

DID YOU KNOW?

The climate impacts the sex of some reptile eggs. For many turtles, warmer nests produce more females.

REPTILES AS PREDATORS

Most reptiles eat insects or other animals, although some also eat plants. Meat-eating reptiles tend to be skilled predators. Snakes, for instance, are usually able to strike extremely fast and some even use venom to weaken their PREY.

SALTWATER CROCODILE

SALTWATER CROCODILE

This animal is one of nature's fiercest predators. Saltwater crocs can lurk underwater for more than an hour at a time. When they attack, they lunge at speed, breaking their prey's neck or drowning it by rolling it in the water.

Turtles tend to eat fish and insects. Some marine turtles also feed on sponges and jellyfish.

DID YOU KNOW?

Lizards mainly eat insects, eggs and plants, though larger lizards might eat bigger prey such as birds.

Snakes are carnivores, which means they only eat other animals. This includes smaller animals like insects, mice, lizards, frogs and snails, as well as other snakes and eggs. Some snakes also eat much bigger animals, such as birds and cats.

A CARPET PYTHON EATING A RODENT

A KOOKABURRA EATING A SNAKE

REPTILES AS PREY

Some reptiles are predators, but many are also prey for kookaburras, eagles and other birds. These flying creatures swoop down from the sky to catch lizards and snakes before the reptiles have a chance to hide.

DEFENCE

Turtles have hard shells to keep predators away, but they are still sometimes attacked by crocodiles or sharks.

Lizards and snakes are also often the victims of cats in search of a meal. Cats are an introduced species, so it is important to minimise their impact on Australian wildlife. Pet cats should be kept inside at night, so they don't attack native species.

Reptiles have developed many clever ways of avoiding predators or scaring them away. If threatened, the frilled lizard will fan out the frill around its head, open its mouth wide and raise its body, so it looks large and scary.

SNAKES

Australia has more than 200 species of snake.
Most of them live on land, but some live in the water.
Some snakes give birth to live offspring, while others lay eggs.

CARPET PYTHON

Many snakes eat rodents, lizards, frogs and even other snakes. Bigger snakes can also eat **MAMMALS** such as wallabies. All snakes are carnivorous, which means they only eat meat.

When they're not basking, snakes spend a lot of time in burrows or under rocks. The earth keeps them warm and hidden from predators.

DID YOU KNOW?

When a person's mouth is full of food, they can only breathe through their nose. A snake can breathe through its mouth when it is eating – because its windpipe sticks out of the bottom of its mouth.

VENOMOUS SNAKES

INLAND TAIPAN

The inland taipan, also called the fierce snake, lives in the outback, hiding in deep cracks in the ground. It is the most venomous snake in the world. Although its venom is very powerful and capable of killing adult humans, it mostly only uses it to catch small animals like rats, and it very rarely encounters people.

COMMON DEATH ADDER

The death adder is found in most of eastern Australia, and along the coast in the southern states. It only grows to about 65cm in length but has the longest fangs of any Australian snake. To attract prey, it sits motionless in leaves or sand and twitches the end of its tail, which looks like a worm.

TIGER SNAKE

When threatened, this highly venomous snake flattens its neck and strikes its prey close to the ground. Adult tiger snakes usually grow to about 1.2m in length and often have stripes that can be pale-yellow to black. Being bitten by one can cause paralysis and breathing difficulties.

Some snakes have special glands in which they make a type of poison called venom. They can deliver this venom by biting down on a victim, using their sharp fangs. Australia is home to more venomous snakes than any other country in the world. Snakebite deaths in humans are rare – you are more likely to be killed by a dog or a cow than a snake.

RED-BELLIED BLACK SNAKE

This snake has red scales on its belly and a black, shiny back. It lives in the bush across eastern and south-eastern Australia, usually near rivers and creeks. It is somewhat less venomous than many other Australian snakes, but you're more likely to come across it in urban areas. A bite from a red-bellied black can cause significant illness.

STAYING SAFE

If you see a snake in the wild, don't panic. Back away slowly to a safe distance. Snakes only bite if they feel threatened.

RED-BELLIED BLACK SNAKE

FRESHWATER TURTLES

There are about 23 kinds of freshwater turtle living in and near Australia's creeks, dams, lakes and rivers. Freshwater turtles include both long-necked and short-necked species. Many turtles can pull their heads and legs inside their shells to protect themselves. Others have long necks they can pull in sideways.

MARY RIVER TURTLE

Mary River turtles begin life as tiny hatchlings of 3–4cm but grow to be one of Australia's largest freshwater turtle species. It often looks like they have a green mohawk because strands of green algae can grow on their heads and shells.

DID YOU KNOW?
A turtle's shell is part of its **SKELETON**. The shell is called a carapace.

Many of Australia's turtles are now threatened or endangered because of challenges like habitat loss, pollution and predation by introduced animals such as foxes. Species such as the Manning River helmeted turtle, the pig-nosed turtle and the Bellinger River snapping turtle are all at risk.

Even though these air-breathing reptiles seem slow on land, sea turtles are perfectly suited for marine habitats. Adults swim through the water at speeds of up to 25 km/h and come up to breathe every 30 minutes.

MARINE TURTLES

There are seven types of sea turtles that live throughout the world's oceans – the green, hawksbill, flatback, loggerhead, leatherback, olive ridley and Kemp's ridley turtles. All but Kemp's ridley turtle swim in Australian waters.

DID YOU KNOW?
Some turtles live to be over 100 years old.

Most female sea turtles return to the same beach where they hatched to lay their own eggs. Once the eggs are laid, the mother returns to the ocean. After about two months, the baby turtles begin to hatch and make their way to the water.

LITTLE LIZARDS

Five lizard families in Australia contain small lizards. Skinks are our most common lizard, and Australia has more species than any other country. Geckos are small, nocturnal lizards with specialised toes that help them grip and climb. Flap-footed lizards, which are also called legless lizards, are often confused with snakes.

Most lizards live on the ground, but some make their homes in trees or burrows.

A gecko's eyes are very sensitive to light. They can see in full colour at night, even when there isn't much light from the Moon.

LIZARDS OR SNAKES

Unlike snakes (and some larger lizards), legless lizards don't have forked tongues. They often have visible ears, which snakes don't have.

The lined fire-tailed skink is thought to wave its fiery tail to communicate with other skinks.

DID YOU KNOW?

Different types of lizards eat many different foods. Most eat insects, including flies and crickets. Others eat leaves, fruits and flowers, or even mammals, birds and other reptiles.

BIG LIZARDS

Australia is home to some seriously large lizards, including species of monitor lizards – also known as goannas – and species of dragons. These reptiles have a prehistoric look to them – monitors evolved from creatures that lived 90 million years ago. More than 90 dragon species live across most of Australia, from coastal cities to central deserts.

GOULD'S MONITOR

Australia's largest monitor is the perentie, growing up to 2.5m long and weighing up to 20kg. The fourth-largest species of lizard in the world, the perentie can run at speeds of up to 40 km/h and stand up on its hind legs to get a better view of its surroundings. Unlike most lizards, it has a forked tongue like a snake.

THORNY DEVIL

The slow-moving thorny devil eats only small black ants, one at a time. It can consume more than 1000 ants in a sitting.

EASTERN WATER DRAGON

DRAGONS

Dragons are related to iguanas and chameleons. They share the unique habit of grabbing food with their tongues. All dragons eat insects, although the larger varieties also eat grass, flowers and other vegetation.

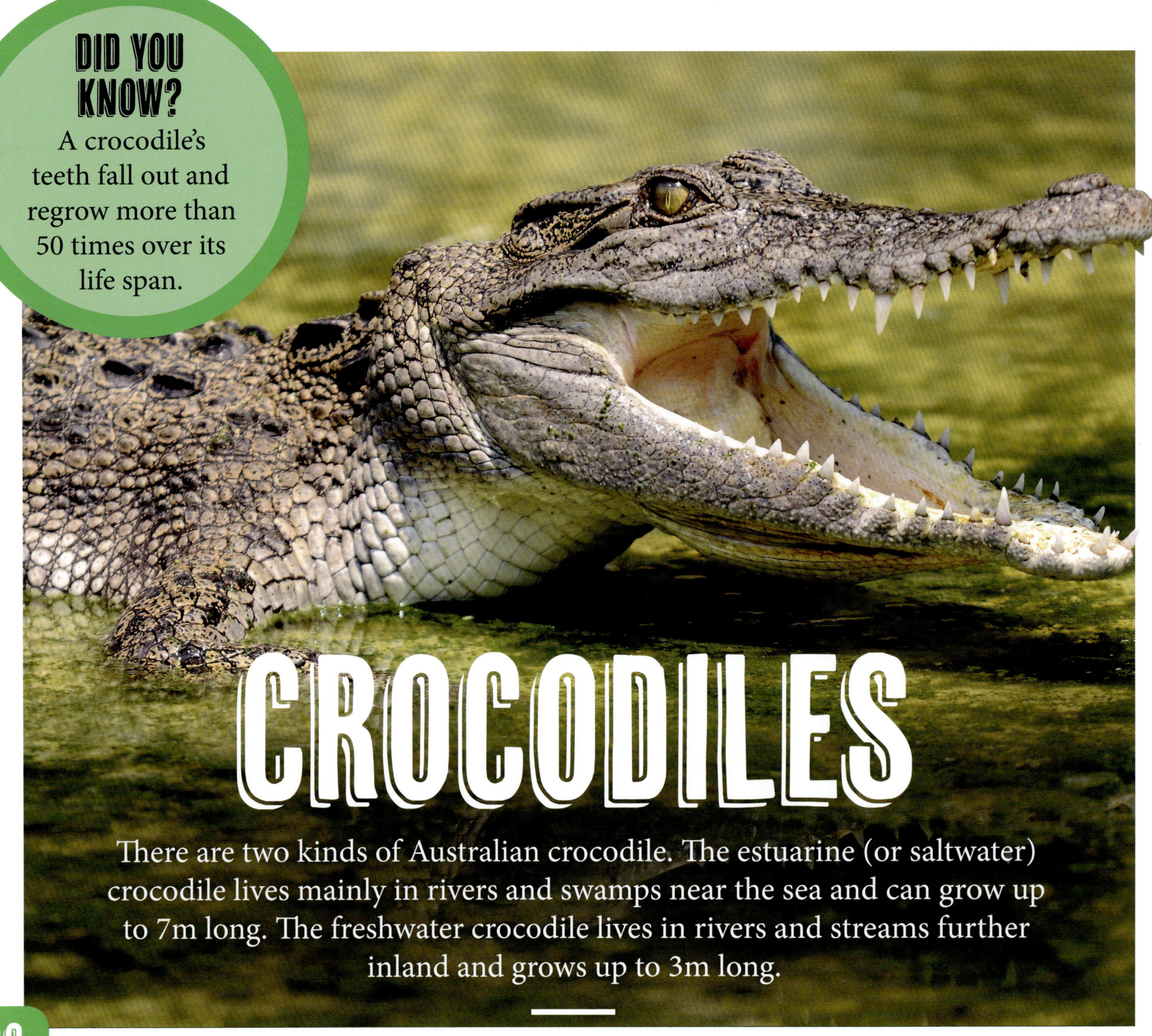

DID YOU KNOW?

A crocodile's teeth fall out and regrow more than 50 times over its life span.

CROCODILES

There are two kinds of Australian crocodile. The estuarine (or saltwater) crocodile lives mainly in rivers and swamps near the sea and can grow up to 7m long. The freshwater crocodile lives in rivers and streams further inland and grows up to 3m long.

If a crocodile catches a small animal, it swallows it whole. If a crocodile catches something bigger, it drags it into deep water and holds it under to drown it before ripping it into pieces to eat.

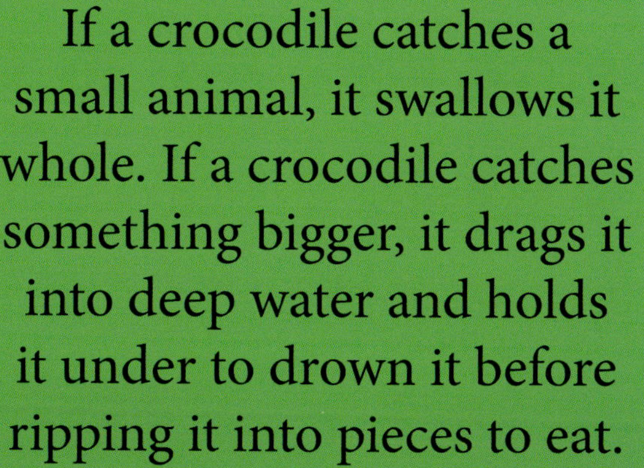

Crocodiles have very strong jaws. They eat a variety of foods, including small mammals, birds and even farm animals. They can leap out of water to reach their prey.

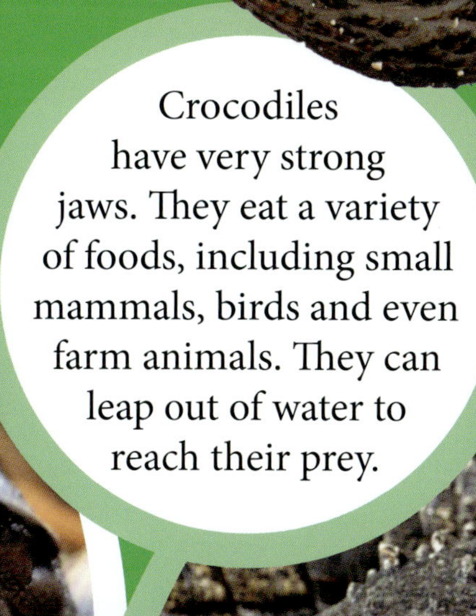

When she's ready to lay her eggs, a female crocodile makes a nest on land. She lays between 50 and 80 eggs in the nest and covers them with leaves, branches or sand. The mother guards the nest for 90 days until the eggs hatch. Once the babies hatch, she uses her mouth to carry them to the water.

OUR REPTILE PAST

Reptiles have lived in Australia for millions of years, all the way back to the time when dinosaurs roamed the Earth. We know about creatures from so long ago because we have found preserved remains of things like bones and feathers – called fossils.

KRONOSAURUS

Australia was once partially covered by an inland sea, which was home to marine reptiles such as ichthyosaurs, plesiosaurs, mosasaurs and sea turtles.

All plesiosaurs had four flippers but could have two different body types – large heads with small necks or small heads with long necks.

DID YOU KNOW?

Umoonasaurus would have been about 2.5m in length.

Some **ANCIENT** land-based reptiles are called dinosaurs. Evidence of Australian dinosaurs has been found from the southern tip of Victoria up to Queensland and across to the edge of Western Australia.

Mosasaurs were long-bodied predators, related to snakes and monitor lizards. They appeared at about the time ichthyosaurs became extinct and the inland sea retreated.

Leaellynasaura was a plant-eating dinosaur that had a long tail, more than twice the length of its body. A skull found in Victoria shows it had a large brain and large eyes.

GLOSSARY

ANCIENT
Belonging to an earlier period in history; very old.

ECTOTHERMS
Animals that can't easily control their internal temperature so rely on the surrounding temperature to make them hotter or cooler.

LEATHERY
A tough and flexible appearance, like leather.

MAMMALS
Animals that breathe air, have a backbone and (usually) grow hair. Female mammals are able to produce milk.

PREDATORS
Animals that eat other animals.

PREY
An animal that is eaten by other animals.

SKELETON
The bony framework of an animal's body.

THERMOREGULATION
A process by which internal body temperature is maintained despite the outside temperature.

VENOMOUS
A type of snake that weakens its prey by injecting poison.

VERTEBRATE
An animal that has a backbone.

PICTURE CREDITS

Images listed clockwise from top left unless specified otherwise.

AG = Australian Geographic; SS = Shutterstock.com;

US = Unsplash.com; CP = CanvaPro

Front cover: reptiles4all/SS; SanchaiRat/SS; Petlin Dmitry/SS; Paul Looyen/SS; Ken Griffiths/SS; Alexandra Lande/SS; Ken Griffiths/SS; Vitaly Korovin/SS; Jiri Lochman/AG; Rich Carey/SS; Ken Griffiths/SS; Steve Wilson/AG. **1:** Andrew Burgess/SS; cynoclub/SS; Jiri Lochman/AG; Kristina Vackova/SS; Susan Schmitz/SS. **2:** Steve Wilson/AG; fotoslaz/SS. **3:** Lewis Burnett/SS; Robert Keresztes/SS; Chris Watson/SS. **4:** Ken Griffiths/SS. **5:** Steve Wilson/AG; dirkr/SS. **6:** Henner Damke/SS; Living Art by Margie/SS. **7:** Mangogo/SS; Simon G/SS. **8:** Richard Thwaites/AG. **9:** Ken Griffiths/SS; Murray Spence/AG. **10:** Ery Azmeer/SS. **11:** Ken Griffiths/SS. **12:** Paul Pixs/SS. **13:** Luke Shelley/SS; Melih Evren/SS; By PetlinDmitry/SS. **14:** David Hancock/AG. **15:** Esther Beaton/AG; Ken Griffiths/SS; Lienka/SS. **16:** Esther Beaton/AG; Kristian Bell/SS; Alizada Studios/SS; Ken Griffiths/SS. **17:** Rory McGuinness. **18:** robdowner/SS. **19:** Ken Griffiths/SS; Andrew Burgess/SS; reptiles4all/SS. **20:** Isabelle Kuehn/SS. **21:** David Evison/SS; Stephanie Rousseau/SS; Rich Carey/SS. **22:** Kristian Bell/SS; Jiri Lochman/AG. **23:** Steve Wilson/AG; Ken Griffiths/SS; James McKinnon/AG. **24:** Steve Wilson/AG. **25:** Esther Beaton/AG; Murray Spence/AG; Jiri Lochman/AG. **26:** dangdumrong/SS. **27:** Arunee Rodloy/SS; PomInOz/SS; Supermop/SS. **28:** Daniel Eskridge/SS. 29: Xing Lida/AG; Xing Lida/AG; Xing Lida/AG. **30:** Vera Larina/SS; john austin/SS; Chameleon'sEye/SS. **31:** Kristian Bell/SS.

Back cover: Trent Townsend/SS.

Australian Geographic
DISCOVER

BOOKS IN THIS SERIES

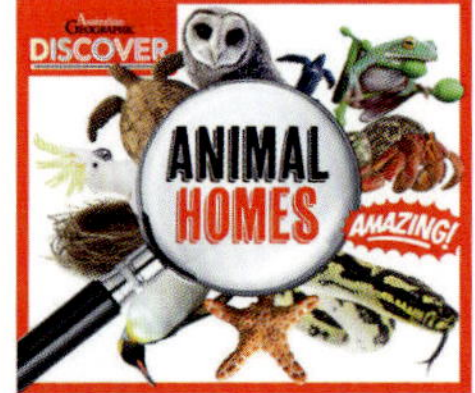

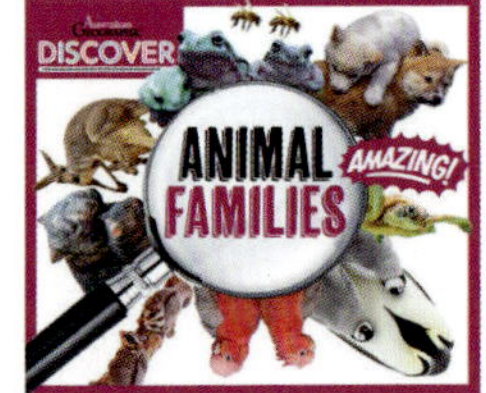

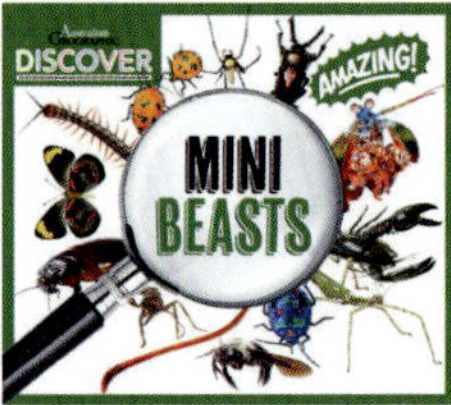

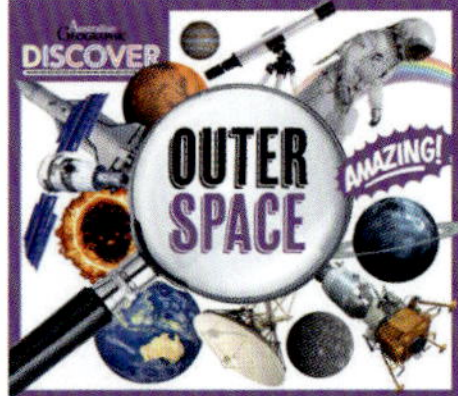

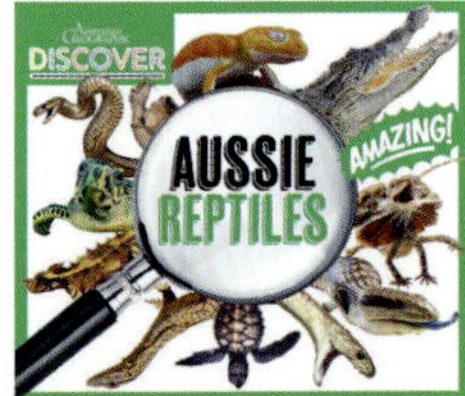

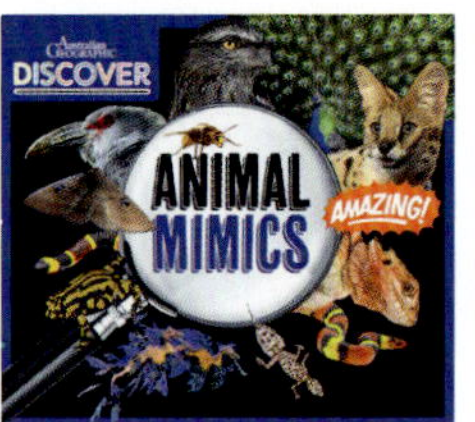

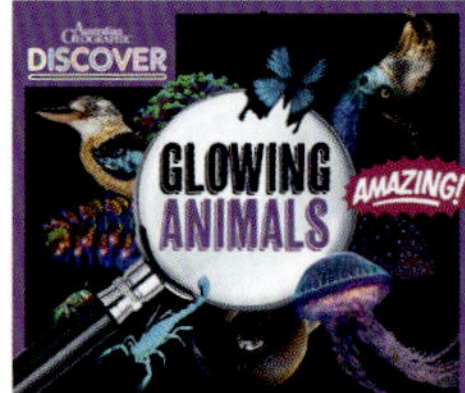

First published in 2020, reprinted in 2023
© Australian Geographic Holdings Pty Ltd
52–54 Turner St, Redfern, NSW

editorial@ausgeo.com.au
australiangeographic.com.au

ISBN: 978-1-925847-75-8

Editor: Lauren Smith
Sub-editors: Rebecca Cotton, Peter Tuskan
Creative director: Mike Elliott
Senior designer: Harmony Southern
Print production: Katrina O'Brien & Andy Franks

AUSTRALIAN GEOGRAPHIC
Managing Director: David Haslingden
Director of Content: Liz Ginis
Licensing and Publishing Manager: Tom Bates
Commercial Assistant: Felicity McManus

Printed in China by C & C Offset Printing Co. Ltd.
The paper in this book is FSC® certified. FSC® promotes environmentally responsible, socially beneficial and economically viable management of the world's forests.

Australian Geographic contributes 100% of its profits to the Australian Geographic Society, including its conservation and sustainability programs.